Seren

The Biography of Tennis' Greatest Female Legends; Seeing the Champion on the Line

By United Library

https://campsite.bio/unitedlibrary

Introduction

Do you love tennis?

If so, this is the book for you. It tells the story of Serena Williams, one of the greatest female tennis players in history. This biography takes an in-depth look at her life and career on and off the court.

Serena Williams is one of the greatest athletes of our time. A dominant force in women's tennis, she has won 23 Grand Slam singles titles, 14 Grand Slam doubles titles, and four Olympic gold medals. In addition to her unparalleled accomplishments on the court, Serena is also an outspoken advocate for social justice and gender equality. She is a powerful role model for young women everywhere, and an inspiration to us all.

Serena was born in 1981 in Saginaw, Michigan, to Richard Williams and Oracene Price. Her father had a background in tennis, and he introduced Serena and her sister Venus to the sport at a young age. The sisters quickly began to dominate the junior tennis circuit, and by the early 2000s they were both ranked among the top ten players in the world.

In 2002, Serena won her first major singles title at the French Open. This was just the beginning of her incredible run of success. Over the next decade, she would go on to win Wimbledon five times, the US Open six times, and the Australian Open three times. She also reached the finals of all four major tournaments on multiple occasions. In total, Serena has appeared in 31 Grand Slams.

You'll learn about all her accomplishments, both personal and professional. Plus, find out what makes her one of the most feared competitors in tennis – and in sports overall. Get a glimpse into her mindset as she strives to be the best that she can be.

Table of Contents

Serena Williams

Serena Williams is an American tennis player born on September 26, 1981 in Saginaw.

Considered one of the greatest players of all time, she has won 39 Grand Slam singles and doubles titles to date: 7 Australian Opens, 3 French Opens, 7 Wimbledons and 6 US Opens in singles; 4 Australian Opens, 2 French Opens, 6 Wimbledons and 2 US Opens in women's doubles with her sister Venus Williams and 1 Wimbledon and 1 US Open in mixed doubles.

By winning her seventh Australian Open on January 28, 2017, Serena Williams becomes with 23 successes the only recordwoman of the number of singles titles won in Grand Slam tournaments during the Open era. She thus overtakes Steffi Graf (22 wins) and is only one win away from Margaret Smith Court's record in the global history of women's tennis. She has also won four Olympic gold medals: three in women's doubles with her older sister Venus (2000, 2008 and 2012) and one in singles won on August 4, 2012 at Wimbledon during the London Olympics. All these results make her the first player in history to have won everything in her career, Grand Slam tournaments and Olympic Games, in singles and doubles.

Over two years in 2002-2003, she won all four Grand Slam tournaments in a row, a performance unseen since Steffi Graf nine years earlier, which earned her the number one ranking in the WTA for 57 consecutive weeks. More irregular from 2004 to 2007 due to injuries and lack of motivation, she regained this ranking on three other occasions, in September 2008 and February 2009, each time with a new Grand Slam victory (at the US Open and the Australian Open), and then from February 2013 in the wake of her Wimbledon-Olympic Games-US Open triple in 2012, a ranking she maintained until September 11, 2016.

By winning Wimbledon in 2016, Serena Williams brings her total number of Grand Slam singles titles to 22 and equals Steffi Graf's record in the Open era. She also achieved for the second time, twelve years apart, the feat of winning the four Majors in a row over two seasons, series called "Serena Slam".

Serena Williams is the younger sister of Venus Williams, who was also ranked number one in the world in 2002. Serena has won nineteen of their thirty-one meetings on Tour since the beginning of 1998. Their meeting in the 2001 US Open final was the first Grand Slam final in the Open era to feature two sisters. They are also the only players to have met in four consecutive Grand Slam finals.

While Serena Williams is at 309 cumulative weeks including 186 consecutive weeks (record co-held by Germany's Steffi Graf) at the top of the WTA rankings, she is dethroned in September 2016 by Germany's Angelique Kerber. She returned to the top of the rankings in January 2017 after her seventh win at the Australian Open, and increased her cumulative time to 319 weeks before ending her season in April, to give birth to the child she is expecting with her fiancé Alexis Ohanian. Their daughter, named Alexis Olympia Ohanian Jr. was born 1er September 2017 and the couple married on November 16, 2017.

Playing style

Her game is based on a very powerful serve and groundstrokes. Serena and her sister were among the first players to use powerful and risky groundstrokes. They also surprised with early forehand and backhand setups. Serena likes to take control of rallies after a good first ball and looks to get the point with a few swings of the racquet. Her serve is considered one of the best in the world because she can hit it hard on the first ball and play very lifted on the second ball, which results in a ball with lots of bite. Her backhand is powerful and often hit flat with a lot of consistency. Her forehand is also very powerful, however, she tends to make a lot of forehand errors at the beginning of the match or when she is under pressure. Her volley is certainly her weak point, although she has improved a lot in the last few years. When necessary, Serena is now able to close the points at the net.

This type of game is great on hard court, but has some difficulties on clay, although it is feared by all players regardless of the surface.

His mental strength has allowed him to get out of complicated situations, as evidenced by winning three grand slams by saving match points (record).

Tennis career

Together with her older sister Venus Williams, she came
from a poor family in Los Angeles and was trained by their
father, who wanted to get them out of their social condition.
He personally coached them on a dilapidated tennis court
from childhood and they began to win their first
tournaments. Serena was born in Saginaw, Michigan, to
Richard Williams and Oracene Price, and was the last of
five siblings: her half-sisters Yetunde, Lindrea and Isha
Price, and her sister Venus. When they were young, the
family moved to Compton, California, where she began
playing tennis at age three. At the U.S. Under-10 level, she
had a record of 46 wins to three losses and was ranked
number one.

WTA Tour debut and first Grand Slam title

Serena Williams made her professional debut at the age of 14 in September 1995 at the Quebec City tournament. However, she failed in the qualifying round, being beaten by her compatriot Annie Miller in a 1-6 doubles match.

She made her return to the circuit in October 1997 when she entered the final draw of a WTA tournament in Moscow for the first time. She was eliminated in the first round by recent Australian Open quarterfinalist Kimberly Po in two sets. Nevertheless, she went on to make the first breakthrough of her career at the Chicago tournament. As a wild card, she faced Elena Likhovtseva in the first round and beat her in two sets 6-3, 7-5. It was her first victory on the WTA Tour. In the second round, she eliminated Mary Pierce, seeded^o 5 and 7^e world player, again in two sets 6-3, 7-6. She continued her journey by eliminating Monica Seles, seeded no.^{o} 4 in the world, in the quarter-finals (4-6, 6-1, 6-1). Then 304^e in the WTA, Serena Williams beats two top 10 and qualifies for the semifinals of the tournament to face Lindsay Davenport, n° 5 world. Her journey ends there, beaten 4-6, 4-6 by her opponent who will win the tournament. She finishes the year for the first time in the top 100, at 99 .^{e}

She starts the 1998 season on the same basis. In Sydney, she qualified for the quarterfinals where she met Lindsay Davenport. This time, Serena Williams takes her revenge and qualifies 1-6, 7-5, 7-5 for her second semi-final. She is dominated by the future winner Arantxa Sánchez Vicario (2-6, 1-6). She then participated in her first Grand Slam tournament, the Australian Open. She was eliminated in the second round by her sister Venus 6^4 -7, 1-6 after having eliminated the top seeded player n° 6 Irina Spîrlea in three sets. She confirmed by reaching the quarter-finals in Miami before logically losing to the world's nº 1 Martina Hingis by pushing her to the tie-break in the third set. She qualified for the quarter-finals again in Rome, losing again to her sister (4-6, 2-6). She reached the round of 16 at the French Open, defeated by Arantxa Sánchez (6-4, 5-7, 3-6), who went on to win the title. She lost in the 3^e round in Wimbledon to Virginia Ruano Pascual. But she won her first Grand Slam title in mixed doubles with Max Mirnyi. The pair went on to win the US Open. She made an impressive progression and finished the year nº 20 in the world at 17 years old.

The 1999 season marked the beginning of a string of titles over the years. After reaching the third round at the Australian Open, eliminated by Sandrine Testud (2-6, 6-2, 7-9), she won her first WTA title at the Open Gaz de France by eliminating no less than 4 Frenchwomen, Nathalie Tauziat, Julie Halard-Decugis, Nathalie Dechy and then Amélie Mauresmo in the final 6-2, 3-6, 7-6. She then went on to Indian Wells where she eliminated Lindsay Davenport (6-4, 6-2), seeded No.º 2 and Mary Pierce (7-5, 7-6), seeded No.º 6 before facing Steffi Graf, seeded No.º 5 in the final. Serena broke in the third set, but managed to take the match and win in three sets (6-3, 3-6, 7-5) in what remains one of the few meetings between the two most successful Grand Slam players of the Open era. She continued her undefeated streak by reaching the final in Miami, defeating Seles nº 3 (6-2, 6-3) and Hingis nº 1 (6-4, 7-6). After winning 16 matches in a row, she lost again to Venus 1-6, 6-4, 4-6.

In Grand Slam, she disappoints in Roland Garros where she is eliminated in the third round by Mary Joe Fernández. Injured, she does not participate in Wimbledon. However, she returned to form and won the Los Angeles tournament, beating Arantxa Sanchez, Hingis and in the final Julie Halard-Decugis, all in two sets. She then found herself in a good position for the US Open, which she started as seeded no.° 7. She defeated Kimberly Po easily in the first round, before starting to have difficulties on her way, losing each time a set against Kim Clijsters in the third round, Conchita Martínez and the seeded no.° 4, Monica Seles in the quarter. She faced and defeated again the seed n° 2 Lindsay Davenport (6-4, 1-6, 6-4) to qualify for her first Grand Slam final. °In this final, she withstood the pressure on her home court, and managed to beat the world's No. 1 Martina Hingis (6-3, 7-6), thus winning the first Grand Slam tournament of her career.

Grand Slam victories

She began her Grand Slam victories at the US Open, which she won in 1999 against Martina Hingis, who had beaten Venus in the semifinals and thus deprived them of a first 100% Williams final. Then she won the French Open, Wimbledon and the US Open consecutively in 2002. Then she won in Melbourne in January 2003. This is how she completes the *Serena Slam*. She became the ninth woman in history to win all four Grand Slams, but also only the fifth to have won all four prestigious tournaments consecutively. That same year, in 2003, she won the Wimbledon tournament.

It is at the Australian Open, that Serena illustrates herself during the following seasons, since she wins in 2005 against Lindsay Davenport and 2007 against Maria Sharapova. She won her 9^e Grand Slam title at the US Open against the Serbian Jelena Janković in 2008. From 2007-2008, her career benefited from the early retirement of Martina Hingis and especially Justine Henin (a player who was as successful as her at that time, although younger). At the 2009 Australian Open, she won her 10^e Grand Slam title and her second in a row against the Russian Dinara Safina. Then, in early July, she won her eleventh title against her sister at Wimbledon. In 2010, she managed to retain her crown at the Australian Open, beating Justine Henin (briefly out of retirement and returning due to injury). A few months later at Wimbledon, she won the tournament without dropping a set, beating Vera Zvonareva in the final. This is her 13^e Grand Slam singles title.

In 2012, Serena Williams won her 14^e Grand Slam title at Wimbledon beating Agnieszka Radwańska of Poland and her 15^e title at Flushing Meadows against Victoria Azarenka of Belarus. In 2013, Serena Williams n° 1 world wins in the final of the French Open against Maria Sharapova for her 16^e Grand Slam title and at the US Open for her 17^e title against Victoria Azarenka. In 2014, for her 18^e victory, she kept her title at the US Open by beating Caroline Wozniacki. In 2015, she won her 19^e Grand Slam title by defeating Maria Sharapova in two sets at the Australian Open then her 20^e at the French Open by disposing of Lucie Šafářová and finally her 21^e at Wimbledon against Spain's Garbiñe Muguruzat and equals Steffi Graff by winning Wimbledon 2016.

Victories against (and with) sister

When she won the four Grand Slam tournaments consecutively, she had to beat her sister Venus Williams in all four finals.

But their history is not only made of rivalry. In doubles, the two sisters won fourteen Grand Slam titles: French Open in 1999 and 2010, US Open in 1999 and 2009, Wimbledon in 2000, 2002, 2008, 2009, 2012 and 2016 and the Australian Open in 2001, 2003, 2009 and 2010. They achieved the Grand Slam by winning the four tournaments in a row from Wimbledon 2009 to Roland Garros 2010.

So when Serena won Wimbledon in 2002 and the Australian Open in 2003, she had to beat her sister in the singles final on Saturday after winning the doubles with her on Friday.

In 2008, five years after her last Grand Slam victory (doubles), Serena won her third Wimbledon with her sister, while a few hours later she lost the women's singles final to Venus 7-5, 6-4. She also won her second Olympic title in Beijing in August 2008 (eight years after Sydney).

In 2009, six years after her last Australian Open victory, the Williams sisters dominated the women's doubles draw and won their third Australian Open against the pair Ai Sugiyama - Daniela Hantuchová in two sets: 6-3, 6-3. The next day, Serena won the singles title. On July 4, 2009, she won her third Wimbledon 7-6, 6-2 against Venus.

2002 to 2003 - At the top of tennis, Grand Slam over two years and number 1 in the world

Serena Williams begins the 2002 season after a somewhat disappointing 2001 season, although she is 6^e world. Serena reached the final at the Scottsdale tournament, having beaten the top seeded player^o 2 Martina Hingis in three sets, then also defeated in three sets the top seeded player^o 1 Jennifer Capriati, thus gaining confidence for the future.

Towards the end of March, she won the Miami tournament as the top seed^o 8, easily beating (6-4, 6-0) the Swiss Martina Hingis in the quarter, then her sister Venus (6-2, 6-2) in the half, and finally Jennifer Capriati (7-5, 7-6^4), not losing any set of the tournament and confirming her good form.

The American begins her clay court season in Charleston, where she loses in the quarterfinals to Patty Schnyder after being down by one set. Serena then competed in Berlin where she took advantage of Amélie Mauresmo's withdrawal in the quarter-finals to easily reach the final, where she lost (2-6, 6-1, 6^5 -7) to Justine Henin. She continued to play in Rome where she managed to get her revenge in the final against Henin (7-6^6 , 6-4), having previously beaten Anastasia Myskina in the quarter, and Jennifer Capriati (6-2, 3-6, 7-5) in the semi-final in a complicated match.

Serena came to the French Open as one of the favorites to win the title after her good preparation tournaments and as the number 3 seed^o . She played well in her first three matches before meeting the Russian Vera Zvonareva in the round of 16, which she beat despite losing the first set

(4-6, 6-0, 6-1). In the quarters, she dominated (6-1, 6-1) the Frenchwoman Mary Pierce, then struggled in the semifinals against the title holder and seeded No.° 1, Jennifer Capriati. She finally won her match (3-6, 7-6^2, 6-2) and qualified for her first French Open final. She faced her sister Venus Williams, seeded no.° 2, whom she managed to beat (7-5, 6-3) in 1 hour and 31 minutes despite a tight first set, winning the 2e Grand Slam tournament of her career and the first at Roland Garros.

She won the Wimbledon tournament by beating in the final again Venus Williams, seeded n° 1, (7-6^4, 6-3). Having dominated her part of the draw, in the quarter against Daniela Hantuchová (6-3, 6-2) and in the semifinals, Amélie Mauresmo seeded n° 9, (6-2, 6-1).

For the last Grand Slam tournament at the US Open, she is again seeded° 1. She easily qualifies for the semifinals where she faces Lindsay Davenport, seeded° 4, whom she beats (6-3, 7-5) and reaches the final without losing a set. She defeated her sister Venus, seeded No.° 2, again (6-4, 6-3). She wins her 3^e Grand Slam title of the season, and the second one at Flushing Meadows after the 1999 edition.

Then, in two weeks, she won two tournaments in Tokyo by beating Kim Clijsters in the final (2-6, 6-3, 6-3), then in Leipzig by beating Justine Henin in the semifinals (6-4, 6-2) and finally (6-3, 6-2) in the final against Anastasia Myskina of Russia.

For the last tournament of her rich season, she participated in the Masters. As the top seed, she defeated Jennifer Capriati in the semifinals in three sets but lost (5-7, 3-6) to Kim Clijsters.

She finished the year for the first time at the 1re world ranking, which marked the beginning of the Williams sisters' reign.

She began the 2003 season as the top seed at the Australian Open° . She struggled in the first round against France's Emilie Loit but eventually won in three sets (3-6, 7-6^5 , 7-5). This difficult victory allowed her to play serenely afterwards. She dominated her opponents until the semi-finals. In the semifinals, she faced Belgian Kim Clijsters, who had beaten her at the Masters. The American defeated her (4-6, 6-3, 7-5) with great difficulty and qualified for the final where she faced the top seeded player° 2 Venus Williams. She defeated her (7-6^4 , 3-6, 6-4) in an equally complicated match, showing her strength of character and her thirst for the title. She wins the title for the first time in Melbourne, and offers herself a Grand Slam achieved over two years.

In February at the Open Gaz de France, she made it to the final, beating France's Amélie Mauresmo in two straight sets. Towards the end of March, she managed to retain her title at the Miami tournament, losing only one set in the final (4-6, 6-4, 6-1) against her compatriot, Jennifer Capriati, in a rather close match, while throughout the tournament Serena was unraveling against her opponents.

The American began her clay court season in Charleston as she had the previous year, advancing to the finals by eliminating Lindsay Davenport, but losing in two sets to Justine Henin. She did not compete in Berlin, but entered Rome where she reached the semifinals and lost to Amelie Mauresmo in three sets.

Then title holder at Roland Garros, she easily won her first matches, taking her revenge of Rome against Mauresmo in the quarter, but lost (2-6, 6-4, 5-7) in the semi-finals in a complicated match against the Belgian Justine Henin, future winner.

Finally for her last tournament of the year due to an injury that forces her to withdraw for the rest of the season, she participates in the defense of her title at Wimbledon as the top seed° 1. She beats first Elena Dementieva in the eighth round, then again Jennifer Capriati (2-6, 6-2, 6-3) and in the semifinals Justine Henin, seeded° 3, (6-3, 6-2) easily enough to reach the final. There, she faced again her sister Venus Williams, seeded n° 2, whom she defeated (4-6, 6-4, 6-2) in a fierce battle, especially in the first two sets, thus winning her second Wimbledon title.

Decline on the circuit 2004 to 2006

Serena, who underwent surgery on her left knee in 2003, has gradually changed her priorities, going from a life totally dedicated to tennis to a much more *fashionable* or showbiz attitude that has never ceased to make people talk.

She will start the 2004 season, winning rather easily the Miami tournament, ousting Maria Sharapova and pulverizing (6-1, 6-1) in the final Elena Dementieva.

At the French Open, when she was seeded second, she lost in the quarter-finals (3-6, 6-2, 3-6) to her compatriot Jennifer Capriati.

She reached the final at Wimbledon by crushing all the competition, getting her revenge in the quarter (6-1, 6-1) against Capriati, then having more difficulties as she lost her first set of the tournament (6^4 -7, 7-5, 6-4) but managed to win against Amelie Mauresmo. She lost badly (1-6, 4-6) against the new tennis super star, the Russian Maria Sharapova, just 17 years old.

During this period, she remains a key player in the tennis world. Her quarter-final match at the US Open in 2004 against Jennifer Capriati (6-2, 4-6, 4-6) was notable for its many unfavorable refereeing decisions. Three gross refereeing errors occurred in the last game alone as Jennifer Capriati served at 5-4 for the match. Clearly Serena should have tied the match at 5-all, which would have put the match back on track. Jennifer Capriati will half-heartedly acknowledge the forfeit in the final interview. Serena will feel robbed, and the chair umpire of the match will be excluded from the New York fortnight. This match has contributed greatly to the implementation of video refereeing in tennis.

In September, she won the Beijing tournament by beating Svetlana Kuznetsova in three sets. Finally, at the Los Angeles Masters, she lost only one match in the pool against Lindsay Davenport (6-3, 5-7, 1-6), which did not prevent her from reaching the semifinals, where she defeated France's Amélie Mauresmo (4-6, 7-6^2 , 6-4) in a very close match. She will be defeated in three sets (6-4, 2-6, 4-6) again by Maria Sharapova who had beaten her at Wimbledon.

Her media gaps, however, did not prevent her from winning an improbable title in Melbourne in 2005 against number 1 seed Lindsay Davenport (2-6, 6-3, 6-0) in the final. Having beaten the number 2 seed Amelie Mauresmo (6-2, 6-2) in the quarterfinals, then in the semifinals in a titanic match of 159 minutes against Maria Sharapova, number 4 seed, finishes in the end of the suspense (2-6, 7-5, 8-6) which will mark her great return to the Grand Slam, when she was down 2-6, 4-5.

But then she accumulated forfeits, fines ($400,000 so far) and excess weight. "I need more time to play at my best" she says to those who question her ambitions on the circuit.

In 2006, she came to defend her title at the Australian Open without any preparation matches and fell in the 3^e round to Daniela Hantuchová (1-6, 6^5 -7). Her ranking dropped below 50^e and she withdrew from the tournaments in Antwerp, Dubai and Miami. After withdrawing from the Charleston tournament (Tier I), she drops out of the top 100 for the first time in almost nine years. She announced shortly thereafter that she would not compete at the French Open or Wimbledon due to a chronic knee injury. She announced her return for the end of the summer, citing doctors' orders.

Back on the circuit (July 2006)

Serena competed in the Cincinnati Open in July, which was her return to the tour. She won her first three matches quite easily, (6-2, 6-2) against Anastasia Myskina (number 2 seed and 10^e in the world) in the first round, then (6-3, 6-1) against Bethanie Mattek in the second round; (6-2, 6-2) against Amy Frazier in the quarterfinals, before falling (2-6, 3-6) to Vera Zvonareva in the semifinals, the eventual winner. The comeback win bodes well for Serena, who despite her semifinal loss, proved to the tennis world that she is still capable of winning matches, including one against a top 10 player.

These results allow her to jump 31 places in the WTA ranking. From 139e she climbs to 108e . Then she reached the semi-finals again at the Los Angeles tournament, where she lost to Jelena Janković. At the US Open, Serena received a *wild-card* and was eliminated in the 4e round by Amélie Mauresmo (world No.^{o} 1) (4-6, 6-0, 2-6), after beating Daniela Hantuchová 7-5, 6-3 and Ana Ivanović 6-4, 6-2 in the 2e and 3e rounds. Note that in the first set of her match against Hantuchová, Serena was down 5-2 before winning the next 5 games and the set. She is now ranked 87e in the world. She decided not to play the end of the season to heal some injuries.

2007 - Back to the highest level

Without a title since her victory in Melbourne in 2005, Serena is more assiduous and participates in the Hobart tournament, a preparation for the Australian Open. She was eliminated in the quarters by the modest Sybille Bammer (6-3, 5-7, 3-6).

In January 2007, Serena Williams participated in the Australian Open, and won the 8^e Grand Slam title of her career in singles, on 3^e in Melbourne. During the fortnight, she plays a dream tennis by beating in the eighth Jelena Janković (6-3, 6-2), coming close to elimination (3-6, 6-2, 8-6) in the quarter against Shahar Peer, then the number 10 seed Nicole Vaidišová (7-6^5 , 6-4). Finally, she won the final against Maria Sharapova, the number 1 seed, whom she beat in 63 minutes (6-1, 6-2). She marks her return to the highest level, reaching after her success the 14^e world ranking, and shows that she is not yet a "finished" player as many claimed.

Similarly, on April 1er , she won the Miami tournament by saving two match points against Justine Henin in the final (0-6, 7-5, 6-3), not without having previously swept Maria Sharapova in the eighth round (6-1, 6-1): she won her 4^e title on the island of Key Biscayne and the 28^e of her career.

The American began her clay court season in Charleston, where she was forced to retire in her first match against Chan Yung-jan, when she was down 3-5 in the first set due to an adductor injury.

Serena appears to be recovered to play the first round of the Fed Cup against Belgium alongside her sister Venus Williams. The younger sister gave the U.S. a point by defeating Caroline Maes in two sets 6-1, 6-4. Serena will not be able to play her second match due to injury.

Serena also gave up playing in Berlin because of her groin injury but went to Rome where she was defeated in three sets by Patty Schnyder (3-6, 6-2, 6^5 -7) in the quarterfinals.

Serena is one of the favorites to win the French Open. In the 1er round, the American struggled against the young Bulgarian Tsvetana Pironkova, however, winning in 3 sets 5-7, 6-1, 6-1. The 2^e round will be more convincing against Milagros Sequera, as she will win in two sets 6-0, $7-6^3$ despite a good resistance from the Venezuelan. In the 3^e round, Serena had some difficulties but finally got through in two sets against the Dutch Michaëlla Krajicek 6-3, 6-4.She played in the round of 16 against the Russian Dinara Safina, whom she beat in two sets (6-2, 6-3), but lost in the quarterfinals to the Belgian Justine Henin in two sets (4-6, 3-6), the Belgian who had no difficulty during the Paris fortnight. Serena will declare that she has never played so badly in a Grand Slam quarterfinal.

She was also beaten in the quarters by the same Justine Henin at Wimbledon (4-6, 6-3, 3-6) and at the US Open (6^3 -7, 1-6), but being injured and arriving without preparation, she could not play the tennis she is known for, while not accepting these defeats.

At the Moscow tournament, she reached the final having beaten Kuznetsova but lost (7-5, 1-6, 1-6) to Elena Dementieva.

In November: the Masters in Madrid: Serena gives up with an injury in the middle of the 1er match. She is replaced by the 10^e , the French Marion Bartoli, who will be beaten 6-0, 6-0 by Justine Henin.

2008 - A return to the forefront and the number one position regained

At the Australian Open, she reached the quarterfinals where she lost 3-6, 4-6 to Serbia's Jelena Janković, world number 4.

She then won back-to-back tournaments in Bangalore against Patty Schnyder and in Miami, beating Janković in the final (6-1, 5-7, 6-3), after beating Justine Henin in the quarterfinals and Svetlana Kuznetsova in the semifinals in three sets, equaling the record of five trophies previously held by Germany's Steffi Graf in the same tournament.

She continued her winning ways and won the Charleston tournament for the first time in her career, beating the Russian Vera Zvonareva in the final in three sets (6-4, 3-6, 6-3), thus becoming an important outsider for the Porte d'Auteuil title. After thirteen consecutive victories, she lost in the quarter-finals in Berlin, defeated in the tie-break of the third set to Dinara Safina (6-2, 1-6, 6^5 -7), the future winner of the tournament. Then in Rome, she withdrew before her quarter-final match against qualifier Alizé Cornet, and in Paris, she lost in the third round to Slovenian Katarina Srebotnik (4-6, 4-6).

At Wimbledon, Serena lost the final to her sister Venus 5-7, 4-6, but had not lost a set before reaching the final. She won the doubles title with her sister on the same day.

Back on the circuit for the Stanford tournament, Serena retired from her semifinal match against Aleksandra Wozniak due to a knee injury. She came up short in her preparation for the Olympics, the only event she had never won in singles. After two convincing first rounds, she suffered against France's Alizé Cornet (3-6, 6-4, 6-4), then lost in the quarter-finals to future Olympic gold medalist Elena Dementieva (6-3, 4-6, 3-6). However, she won another gold medal in doubles with her sister, as in Sydney in 2000.

The US Open starts with a new fact: 6 players can become n° world at the end of this tournament, including Serena, ranked 3^e . Already a double winner in New York, she easily qualifies for the quarterfinals, where she meets Venus for their 18^e confrontation. Serena won in two very tight sets ($7-6^6$, $7-6^7$) in a very intense match. Serena saved 10 set points against her sister. In the semifinals, Serena easily beat Dinara Safina (6-3, 6-2). In the final, she won the title by defeating (6-4, 7-5) Jelena Janković, against whom she had lost in the quarters at the Australian Open. This victory allows her to become number 1 in the world again on September 8, five years after leaving this position. With this 9^e Major, she also becomes the 8^e most titled Grand Slam player in history, *tied* with Maureen Connolly and Monica Seles. She announced after this title that she wants to reach double digits in Grand Slam in 2009.

She made her return to competition at the Stuttgart tournament where she lost in the first round to the surprise of everyone against Li Na by the score of 6-0, 1-6, 4-6. She loses her world number 1 ranking to Jelena Jankovic, the future winner of the event.

Following a minor knee injury, Serena would not return to competition until the Doha Masters. She won her first match easily against Dinara Safina (6-4, 6-1) but was then defeated by her sister 7-5, 1-6, 0-6. Following this defeat, she withdrew due to an abdominal injury, ending the year with a forfeit like the previous year. She finishes the 2008 season as the world's number 2.

2009 - Best season since 2002-2003 and richest player in history

Serena Williams starts the year in Sydney. She lost in the semifinals to eventual winner Elena Dementieva (3-6, 1-6) after saving match points in the first round against Samantha Stosur (6-3, 6^4 -7, 7-5) and in the quarter against Caroline Wozniacki (6^5 -7, 6-3, 7-6^3). She then won the Australian Open for the fourth time in her career. After three easy rounds, she was upset by the Belarusian Victoria Azarenka, who won the first set 6-3 but had to retire in the second set due to a severe sunstroke. In the quarters, she was almost eliminated when she was defeated 5-7, 3-5 by Svetlana Kuznetsova, but she finally won 5-7, 7-5, 6-1. In the semifinals, she met Dementieva again and this time, Serena took her revenge by winning (6-3, 6-4). In the final, she met Dinara Safina in search of her first Grand Slam win, but the match was short-lived as Serena won 6-0, 6-3 in less than an hour. In addition to winning her 10^e Grand Slam tournament, she also became the world's No. 1 player after this tournament.

She followed up with two semifinals at the Open Gaz de France (forfeit) and then in Dubai (loss to her sister Venus): 1-6, 6-2, 6^3 -7, future winner. Absent from Indian Wells, a tournament she has boycotted since 2001, she made her return to Miami, a tournament she has already won five times. After a difficult run with victories in three sets over Zheng Jie (7-5, 5-7, 6-3), Li Na (4-6, 7-6^1 , 6-2) and her sister Venus (6-4, 3-6, 6-3), she lost in the final to Victoria Azarenka in a match where Serena had injured her left thigh.

Her season on European clay courts was catastrophic as she did not win a single match in three tournaments. At the French Open, she reached the quarterfinals, but lost to eventual winner Svetlana Kuznetsova after a hard-fought match (6^3 -7, 7-5, 5-7).

At Wimbledon, she easily passed the first rounds and then took her revenge on Azarenka in the quarters (6-2, 6-3). In the semifinals, she had to save match points against Elena Dementieva, but she won with a strong finish and mental strength 6^4 -7, 7-5, 8-6. In the final, she meets her sister, who is the double title holder. She took her revenge on last year's final (7-6^3 , 6-2), thus winning her third Wimbledon title. She completes this success with a victory in doubles alongside her sister.

After an average American tour for her status, she arrives at the US Open, where she easily qualifies for the semi-finals. She met Kim Clijsters, who made her return to competition during the summer after an absence due to maternity. Clijsters won in two sets (4-6, 5-7) against a Serena at her best, although the match was marked by an incident that led to Serena's elimination after a penalty point· .

At the Beijing tournament, she lost in the 3^e round to Nadia Petrova. She went on to win the Masters for the second time in her career after defeating Venus Williams (6-2, 7-6^4) in the final, having won all her previous matches. With this success, the younger of the Williams sisters became the highest earning female tennis player of her career. She also takes over the world No. 1 ranking from Dinara Safina and ends the year at the top of the rankings for the first time since 2002. With two Grand Slam singles titles and three doubles titles, Serena Williams becomes the first player since Martina Hingis in 1999 to be named world champion in both singles and doubles.

2010 - The Williams sisters at the top

As in the previous season, Serena Williams started with the Sydney tournament, where she lost clearly to Elena Dementieva (3-6, 2-6) in the final, after almost losing in the semifinals to Aravane Rezaï of France, whom she defeated 3-6, 7-5, 6-4 after being down 3-6, 2-5.

At the Australian Open, she made it to the quarter-finals, where she met Victoria Azarenka. After being dominated for a set and a half (4-6, 0-4 for the Belarusian), she turned the tables and ended up winning 4-6, 7-6^4 , 6-2. In the semifinals, she overcame Li Na after two tie-breaks. In the final, she met up with the returning Justine Henin for her fourteenth encounter with the Belgian player, but her first in a Grand Slam final. By winning her duel with Henin (6-4, 3-6, 6-2), Serena clinched her twelfth major title, matching Billie Jean King. Alongside her sister Venus, she also retained her doubles title, defeating the world's number one pair Black-Huber in two sets (6-4, 6-3). She also became the first player since Martina Navrátilová to win at least one Grand Slam title in three different decades in both singles and doubles.

With a knee injury, she will be absent from the circuit for nearly three months. She will not play in Paris, Dubai, Miami, Charleston and Marbella.

Serena Williams makes her return to the circuit in Rome, where she reaches the semifinals. However, she loses at this stage against Jelena Janković with a score of 4-6, 6-3, 7-6^5 in favor of the Serb, who had to erase match points in the process. In Madrid, Serena Williams plays, in the second round, the longest match of her career by eliminating the Russian Vera Dushevina (6^2 -7, 7-6^5 , 7-6^5) after 3h26. However, she lost in the round of 16 to Nadia

Petrova, 6-4, 2-6, 3-6. She also took part in this tournament in doubles with her sister to prepare for the French Open. The pair triumphed without dropping a set and as a result are ranked No.$^\circ$ 2 in the world, their final opponents being the No. 8 seeded team of Gisela Dulko and Flavia Pennetta.

At the French Open, Serena Williams was eliminated in the quarter-finals by Samantha Stosur, who had beaten Justine Henin in the previous round, by a score of 2-6, 7-6[2], 6-8. Thanks to her victory in the women's doubles final, she and her sister Venus are now ranked number one in the world in doubles at the end of the second round of the Grand Slam .

On July 4, she won for the fourth time the Wimbledon tournament by beating (6-3, 6-2) the Russian Vera Zvonareva, and after having beaten the Chinese Li Na, seeded number 9, in the quarter (7-5, 6-3) and then Petra Kvitová in the semifinals, also in two sets .

Following a foot injury in early July (broken glass in a restaurant), Serena Williams is forced to withdraw from the entire U.S. tour and the final Grand Slam of the season. However, the defeat of Caroline Wozniacki in the semifinals of the US Open allowed her to keep her world number 1 ranking. She lost her number 1 ranking during the Beijing tournament to Caroline Wozniacki and finished the year at number 4 .[e]

2011 - Medical complications and winning return

Serena Williams has had a difficult start to the 2011 WTA Tour season. Still not having recovered from her injury sustained in July 2010, she was forced to withdraw from the Hopman Cup and the Australian Open, and dropped from 4[e] to 12[e] in the WTA rankings because she was unable to defend her title.

On March 2, Serena Williams was rushed to the hospital with a hematoma following treatment for a pulmonary embolism diagnosed a few days earlier.

It was in June that she announced her return. Like her sister Venus, the two former WTA Tour stars finally found their way back to the courts at the Eastbourne tournament in preparation for Wimbledon. She fell in the second round to Vera Zvonareva, then 3[e] world player, after a match lasting more than three hours.

At Wimbledon, Serena, then title holder, lost in the round of 16 to Marion Bartoli (3-6, 6[6] -7). The American then fell to 175[e] in the WTA rankings in July.

At the Stanford tournament (*Premier Event*) at the end of July 2011, Serena found her usual form. She won her first title since Wimbledon 2010 after dominating Maria Sharapova (6-1, 6-3), Sabine Lisicki (6-1, 6-2) and Marion Bartoli (7-5, 6-1), losing only one set of the tournament.

She confirmed her winning comeback by winning the Canadian Open (*Premier Event 5*) in Toronto a fortnight later against Samantha Stosur (6-4, 6-2), the only player in the top 10 along with Azarenka (in the semis, 6-3, 6-3) whom she had to face during this edition. This is only her second title in the most important Canadian tournament, ten years after her victory over Jennifer Capriati.

At the US Open, Serena eliminated the[oe] top seed Caroline Wozniacki in the semifinals (6-2, 6-4), after beating Victoria Azarenka in the third round (6-1, 7-6[5]) and met up again with Australian Samantha Stosur (10[e]) in the final. But unlike in Toronto two weeks earlier, the American was unable to get her game going and quickly lost her temper, verbally abusing the umpire on several occasions. She lost her 17[e] Grand Slam final in two sets (2-6, 3-6), but improved to 14[e] world ranking in September 2011.

2012 - Quadrupled Wimbledon, Olympics, US Open and Masters singles

She was quite convincing in her first three matches at the Australian Open, but suffered a cruel defeat in the round of 16 (2-6, 3-6) against the Russian Ekaterina Makarova, 56[e] world player.

She then participated in the Miami tournament, where she lost in the quarterfinals (4-6, 4-6) to Caroline Wozniacki.

In Charleston, she easily won the tournament by beating Lucie Šafářová (6-0, 6-1) in the final. This is her fortieth title on the WTA tour.

In Madrid, on the blue clay, she had an impressive week, ousting Caroline Wozniacki (1-6, 6-3, 6-2) and Maria Sharapova (6-1, 6-3) in the quarters, and winning the title over world number one Victoria Azarenka (6-1, 6-3).

In Rome, she continued to impress but withdrew shortly before her semi-final against Li Na of China, suffering from a lower back injury.

At the French Open, she lost after more than three hours of play to Virginie Razzano of France in the first[er] round of the tournament (6-4, 6^5 -7, 3-6). It was her first defeat in the first round of a Grand Slam tournament. Two days after this defeat, she decided to train with the Frenchman Patrick Mouratoglou.

At the Wimbledon tournament, she won her 14[e] Grand Slam title in 3 sets, 6-1, 5-7, 6-2, against the Polish Agnieszka Radwańska 3[e] world. After eliminating the world

4^e Petra Kvitová in the quarter and the world n° 2, Victoria Azarenka (6-3, 7-6^6). On the same day, she won her 5^e Wimbledon in doubles with her sister Venus. This is her 13^e Grand Slam in doubles. During the tournament, she breaks the record for the number of aces for women in a match (24 in the semifinals against Azarenka) and during the tournament (102 in total).

Serena Williams won the Stanford tournament just after winning Wimbledon, beating in the final the American Coco Vandeweghe (7-5, 6-3), a Lucky Loser. This is her forty-third win on the WTA Tour. She joins her sister Venus.

She participates in the Summer Olympics in London and achieves an exceptional record. In the singles tournament, she beats Jelena Janković, number 1 in 2008, in the first round (6-3, 6-1). She then defeats in the 2^e round Urszula Radwańska (6-2, 6-3). In the third round, she faced Vera Zvonareva and won 6-1, 6-0. In the quarterfinals, she meets the former number 1 Caroline Wozniacki which she easily defeats (6-0, 6-3). In the semifinals, she plays against the world number 1, Victoria Azarenka but doesn't give her a chance and wins the match (6-1, 6-2). She then found herself in the final against Maria Sharapova whom she beat (6-0, 6-1). She wins the gold medal of the 2012 Olympic Games. Serena also made a flawless performance in women's doubles, which she played with her sister Venus Williams. They made it to the finals by defeating Romania (Sorana Cîrstea and Simona Halep), Germany (Angelique Kerber and Sabine Lisicki), Italy (Sara Errani and Roberta Vinci) and Russia (Maria Kirilenko and Nadia Petrova) to reach their third Olympic women's doubles final in three appearances. The sisters retain their Olympic title in the women's doubles of the London Games, beating the Czechs Andrea Hlaváčková and Lucie Hradecká in two sets 6-4, 6-4, in Wimbledon. This is the third title for the Williams sisters who had been crowned in Sydney in 2000 and Beijing in 2008, . In addition, she also becomes the first tennis player to win all four Grand Slam tournaments in singles, doubles and Olympic gold in singles and doubles.

At the US Open, Serena Williams defeated all her opponents, without dropping a single set and losing only 19 games in 6 matches (almost 3 games per match on average), before facing the world number 1 Victoria Azarenka in the final. This is the revenge of the last semifinals of the Wimbledon tournament and the London Olympics, in which Serena Williams easily beat the Belarusian player. In the first set, Serena took her opponent's serve to quickly lead 3-0. In the second set, Serena Williams lost 6-2 and was on the verge of defeat when V. Azarenka led 5-3 in the final set. Serena Williams finally managed to win (7-5), thus winning her 4[e] US Open and her 15[e] Grand Slam title. In addition, she becomes the third player of the Open era to win the Wimbledon-JO-US Open triple after Steffi Graf in 1988 and her sister Venus in 2000, .

At the Istanbul Masters, she arrives as a great favorite. She wins her three pool matches, against Angelique Kerber (6-4, 6-1), Li Na (7-6[2] , 6-3) and then the world number 1 Victoria Azarenka (6-4, 6-4), despite a rather disappointing game, with a less efficient service than usual in 2012. In the semis, she easily eliminates Agnieszka Radwańska 6-2, 6-1 in just one hour, before winning her third Masters final by beating Maria Sharapova (6-4, 6-3) in an hour and a half, who still has trouble beating the American.

2013 - Return to world number one and triple Roland Garros, Us Open and Masters singles

Williams begins her season with the Brisbane tournament. She successively swept Varvara Lepchenko (6-2, 6-1), Alizé Cornet (6-2, 6-2), Sloane Stephens (6-4, 6-3) before benefiting from Victoria Azarenka's withdrawal in the semi-finals. She won the tournament by beating Anastasia Pavlyuchenkova (6-2, 6-1) without dropping a set all week.

She arrives as a favorite at the Australian Open. In her first round match, she eliminated Edina Gallovits (6-0, 6-0) but violently twisted her ankle in the first set. In the next round, she ousted Garbiñe Muguruza (injuring her lip in the process by hitting herself with a racket). She then crushed Ayumi Morita (6-1, 6-3) and Maria Kirilenko (6-2, 6-0) to advance to the quarterfinals. For the first time in her career, Williams lost to a younger American player, Sloane Stephens (6-3, 5-7, 4-6) in 2 hours and 17 minutes, after injuring her back once again. . Azarenka's victory in the final prevented her from becoming world number one.

Williams then participated in the tournament in Doha. Despite losing in the final to defending champion and world number one Victoria Azarenka (6^6 -7, 6-2, 3-6), she regained her place at the top of the women's tennis hierarchy. Then, from March 19 to 30, she participated in the Miami Open, which she won for the sixth time in her career after a long final against Maria Sharapova (4-6, 6-3, 6-0) in 2 hours and 8 minutes, thus consolidating her position as world number one. During this week, she will beat Dominika Cibulková in three sets, the number 5 seed Li Na (6-3, $7-6^5$) in 1h50 and Agnieszka Radwańska number 4 seed.This victory of Serena Williams is a new record that the player displays on her roll. In fact, she is the first player to win the Miami tournament six times, surpassing the record of five victories that she held with Steffi Graf.

She then continues on the green clay of the Charleston tournament where she is the title holder. A tournament marked by two matches in one day for Serena and Venus. The two sisters met in the semi-finals and Serena won very easily, leaving only three games to her elder sister. In the final, she beat Jankovic in three sets (3-6, 6-0, 6-2) in 1h55. She wins for the second time in a row in Charleston.

Serena Williams is back on the clay court in Madrid with her position as world number 1 in danger. The American showed a satisfactory level of play beating Yulia Putintseva with a tie-break, Lourdes Domínguez Lino and Maria Kirilenko before facing the Spaniard Anabel Medina Garrigues. A match of great intensity where Williams conceded a 6-0 in the second set but won 7-5 in the third set, coming within two points of defeat at 4-5, 30-30. In the semifinals, she defeated Sara Errani (7-5, 6-2) and met Maria Sharapova in the final with the number one spot at stake. It was the third meeting of the year between the two players, which once again turned to Williams' advantage. She wins in two sets 6-1, 6-4 in 1 hour and 18 minutes, and confirms her place as world number 1.

She then won the Rome tournament against Victoria Azarenka (6-1, 6-3) in 1h33, 11 years after her one and only victory in Rome.

She participated in the French Open, which she won only once, in 2002, against her sister Venus Williams. She easily passed the first round by eliminating the Georgian Anna Tatishvili by 6-0, 6-1, in 51 minutes. In the second round, she defeated Caroline Garcia of France, beat Sorana Cîrstea of Romania in the third round and ousted Roberta Vinci of Italy in the round of 16. In the quarterfinals, she defeated Russian Svetlana Kuznetsova in three sets (6-1, 3-6, 6-3), offering her resistance for the first time in the tournament. In the semifinals, she faced the Italian and fifth player in the world, Sara Errani, whom she dominated 6-0, 6-1 in 46 minutes. She reached the final of the Parisian tournament for the first time in eleven years, where she met the Russian and second player in the world, Maria Sharapova, whom she beat (6-4, 6-4) in one hour and 46 minutes, concluding with an ace at 198 km/h on match point. She wins her second French Open title and her 16e Grand Slam singles title at the age of 31. Serena Williams has now won 31 consecutive matches.

While she seemed destined to win her sixth title on the London grass court, she was surprisingly eliminated in the round of 16 by the top seed°ed German Sabine Lisicki (2-6, 6-1, 4-6), a future finalist who had played an excellent match. She thus stops a series of 34 consecutive victories.

Afterwards, she won two more tournaments. First, in Båstad in mid-July, on clay, she did not lose a set and beat Johanna Larsson in the final. Then, on August 11, she won the Rogers Cup, also without dropping a set in the tournament; with this 54e success, she surpassed Monica Seles in the number of titles won on the WTA Tour.

At the ESPY Awards, Serena Williams is voted best female athlete of the year and best female tennis player of the year.

She then went on to the Cincinnati tournament where she reached the final, where she lost to her runner-up, Azarenka, in the final (6-2, 2-6, 6^6 -7) in two and a half hours of play.

She won the US Open Series ahead of Azarenka and Radwanska.

At the US Open, Williams easily disposed of Schiavone, Voskoboeva and Shvedova. [e]In the round of 16, she got her revenge on her compatriot Sloane Stephens (6-4, 6-1), before crushing Carla Suárez Navarro (6-0, 6-0) and then the world's No. 6, Li Na (6-0, 6-3). She met again with Victoria Azarenka in the final, for a rematch of the 2012 final. She won in three sets (7-5, 6[6] -7, 6-1) after 2h45 of a tense and fierce battle, thus winning her 17[e] Grand Slam and her 5[e] US Open. At the same time, she pocketed a record check of 3.6 million dollars. It is worth noting that Williams blocked Azarenka's path to the title at Flushing Meadows for the third consecutive time .

She wins her 10[e] title of the season by dominating Serbia's Jelena Janković in the final of the WTA tournament in Beijing, 6-2, 6-2. This is the 56[e] tournament won in singles by the younger of the Williams sisters and her third consecutive Premier Mandatory of the season.

Serena Williams completes her season with a Masters title, her fourth. In pool she quietly defeats her opponents who are: Angelique Kerber, Agnieszka Radwańska and Petra Kvitová. In the semifinals she experiences more difficulty, as she loses a set (6-4, 2-6, 6-4) against Jelena Janković in more than two hours, and in the final against Li Na in also two hours (2-6, 6-3, 6-0) and losing a second set. She breaks her own record, being the oldest player to win the Masters in singles, at 32 . This is the best season of her career, with a total of eleven titles won, logically finishing the year at the top of the world rankings. This season, she won 78 of her 82 matches, for a winning percentage of 95.1%.

2014 - 200 weeks in the number 1 spot and 18ᵉ Grand slam

Serena Williams started the year with the Brisbane tournament, where she is the defending champion. °She won the trophy for the second year in a row after defeating Maria Sharapova in the semifinals (6-2, 7-6^7) and world number two Victoria Azarenka in the final (6-4, 7-5). At 32 years old, the American adds a 58ᵉ title to her list of achievements. At the Australian Open, she lost in the round of 16 to Serbian Ana Ivanović, seeded No.° 14, in three sets 6-4, 3-6, 3-6.

She then withdrew from the Doha tournament due to a back injury sustained at the Australian Open.

A week after Doha, Serena Williams takes advantage of a *wild card* to participate in the Dubai tournament. She successively eliminates Ekaterina Makarova and Jelena Janković, but fails in the semi-finals against Alizé Cornet (4-6, 4-6). In a press conference, Serena Williams will say she regrets her participation in the tournament, her back injury is not completely healed.

Serena Williams then begins the tournament in Miami where she is the title holder and wins her 7ᵉ title on the island of Key Biscayne (absolute record men/women combined) by eliminating successively Yaroslava Shvedova, Caroline Garcia (6-4, 4-6, 6-4) of 20 years, the qualified Coco Vandeweghe, Angelique Kerber (6-2, 6-2) seeded number 5 and the seeded number 4, Maria Sharapova while she was led 4-1 in the first set (6-4, 6-3) in 1h37. In the final, she met the world's n° 2 Li Na. Serena Williams started the match very badly until she was down 5-2 in the first set but finally won in two sets 7-5, 6-1 and two hours of play.

Serena Williams begins the clay court season with a crushing defeat in the second round of the Charleston tournament where she was the title holder. Injured in the thigh, she can not do anything against the young Jana Čepelová who wins the match with the score of (4-6, 4-6). Serena Williams declares in a press conference that she will retire from the circuit for a few weeks to take stock of her physical and mental health. Indeed, in the last two years, Serena Williams has been playing a lot of tournaments and she says she is mentally and physically tired.

She made her return to the tournament in Madrid where she is a two-time defending champion. Serena Williams made it through the first rounds, but withdrew from the quarterfinals against Petra Kvitová due to a thigh injury.

The world n° 1 returns to Rome to defend her title. She wins her 60^e title and becomes triple champion of the tournament after her victories in 2002, 2013 and 2014. To achieve this, she defeated Andrea Petkovic, Varvara Lepchenko and Zhang Shuai before meeting Ana Ivanović in the semifinals who had taken her out in January at the Australian Open. Williams takes her revenge in three sets (6-1, 3-6, 6-1) in 1h36. In the final, she met Sara Errani whom she easily beat in two sets 6-3, 6-0 and 1h11.

At the French Open, where she was the favourite and defending champion, she lost in the second round to the young Spaniard Garbiñe Muguruza in two straight sets (2-6, 2-6), which was a big surprise.

At Wimbledon, where she is highly anticipated after her two premature losses at the Australian Open and French Open, she easily defeated Anna Tatishvili in the first^{er} round and Chanelle Scheepers in the second, but fell in the third round to Alizé Cornet (6-1, 3-6, 4-6). This is the 1re time since 2006, that Serena Williams is eliminated three times in a row before the quarterfinals in Grand Slam. And in doubles with her sister Venus, during their second round doubles match, Serena suffered a strange illness that forced her to retire.

Serena then won the Stanford tournament by beating Germany's Angelique Kerber (7-6[1] , 6-3), who was in a bad way in the first set, after losing a set (2-6, 6-3, 7-5) and difficulties against Ana Ivanović in the quarter. In Montreal, she failed in the semifinals against her sister Venus in three sets: 7-6[2] , 2-6, 3-6 in a little over two hours while struggling to put her game together this week. Serena is back to her best in Cincinnati by winning her 62[e] title against Ana Ivanović (6-4, 6-1) in just over an hour. Trailing 3-1 in the first set, she won 7 straight games to win the first set and completely outplayed Ivanović to close out 6-1 in the second. In this tournament, she will still struggle to beat Caroline Wozniacki again in three sets and from her first match against Samantha Stosur concluded in two tie-breaks. Serena went on to win the US Open Series for the third time and will receive a $1 million bonus if she wins at Flushing Meadows. She won the tournament on September 7 (6-3, 6-3 in the final against her friend Caroline Wozniacki, 11[e]) without losing a single set and without any difficulty in crushing the competition' .

As a result, Serena Williams won her sixth US Open (record initially held by Chris Evert), her third in a row and above all her 18e Grand Slam, which makes her the equal of Martina Navratilova and Chris Evert. She pockets a record check of 4 million dollars, 3 for the title at Flushing Meadows plus 1 million bonus from the US Open Series.

In Wuhan, she gave up in her second round match against Alizé Cornet when she was leading by a break of 6-5. Feverish and nauseous, she fell for the third time (this time by withdrawal) to Cornet. This is the first time since Justine

Hénin in 2007 that Serena loses three matches against the same player in the same season.

A few days later in Beijing, she withdrew before her quarter-final against Samantha Stosur due to a knee injury.

She then starts the WTA season-ending Masters in Singapore with a nice win over Serbian Ana Ivanović (6-4, 6-4). But she was surprised in her second pool match where Simona Halep left her only two games (0-6, 2-6). Thus, Serena loses a match for the first time at the Masters since 2008, but more importantly, it is the first time since 1998 that she does not score more than two games in a match that has been to its end. The next day, she found her usual form and clearly beat Eugenie Bouchard in 57 minutes (6-1, 6-1). Combined with the results of the other players in her pool, Serena finally managed to qualify for the semi-finals of the Masters. She met Caroline Wozniacki, who was top of the other group: after a catastrophic start to the match (only 3 of the first 15 points won), the world's n° 1 gradually rectified the situation against an excellent opponent and concluded the match on her 3^e opportunities (2-6, 6-3, 7-6^6) after more than 2 hours of play.

Williams met Halep again in the final on October 26 at the Singapore Indoor Stadium, and took revenge for their first round meeting, winning (6-3, 6-0) in 1 hour and 11 minutes. She is the first to win the Masters for the third consecutive time since Monica Seles (1990-1992).

Serena is named the WTA Women's Player of the Year for the sixth time in her career. In singles, she has 64 titles and finishes her season with $9 million in tournament earnings.

2015 - A "Serena Slam" at two Grand Slam tennis matches

In 2015, Serena Williams begins her season not with a preparation tournament as in the previous three years, but with an exhibition, the Hopman Cup, with a victory over Flavia Pennetta but taking a 6-0, a dry loss to Eugenie Bouchard and a hard-fought victory over Lucie Šafářová, showing her complicated and somewhat worrisome beginning of the year. In doubles with her teammate John Isner, they win all three of their matches. They still qualify for the final but lose 2-1 to the Poles.

She participated in the Australian Open, which she has not won since 2010. She successively eliminated Alison Van Uytvanck, Vera Zvonareva (7-5, 6-0) and Elina Svitolina before meeting the Spaniard Garbiñe Muguruza in the last 16. Serena Williams took revenge for her defeat the previous year at Roland Garros in three sets (2-6, 6-3, 6-2). She then defeated Dominika Cibulková in the quarterfinals (6-2, 6-2) and then took out the young American Madison Keys (7-6^5 , 6-2) in the semifinals. She met again with world number two Maria Sharapova in the final, beating her for the 16^e time in two sets (6-3, 7-6^5). She won her nineteenth Grand Slam tournament and sixth in Melbourne (the most in the Open era), surpassing Martina Navrátilová and Chris Evert in terms of Grand Slam victories (18 each) .

She then participated in the Fed Cup in Argentina but was forced to withdraw after her first match, weakened by a virus contracted in Australia and from which she is still not cured.

In March, Serena Williams played Indian Wells, after 14 years of boycotting the event following the public's whistles during the final, which blamed her for the withdrawal of her sister Venus, against whom she should have played in the semis. She is trying to turn the page and says: "I can't wait to be back on center court to show the world that you don't have to worry about the hostility you may encounter or arouse"[..] . She left the tournament in the semifinals, forfeiting the match because of a sore knee.

During the Miami tournament, she eliminated the young American Catherine Bellis (only 15 years old) in the third round (6-1, 6-1) in less than an hour, then Svetlana Kuznetsova in the next round and in the quarter-finals against the German Sabine Lisicki (7-6,[4] , 1-6, 6-3) in two hours of play and signed there her 700[e] victory on the professional circuit. She then met world number three Simona Halep in the semifinals, winning the match in three sets (6-2, 4-6, 7-5) with great difficulty in just over two hours. In her tenth final at Key Biscayne, she completely dominated Spain's Carla Suárez Navarro (6-2, 6-0) in less than an hour to win her 3[e] straight title and her eighth overall.

In order to prepare for the clay court season, she decided to participate in the Fed Cup but this time without her sister (Venus Williams withdrew a week before the match due to personal problems). Serena won her two matches against Camila Giorgi and Sara Errani but failed in doubles, letting Italy qualify for the world group.

On April 27, she began her 115[e] consecutive weeks at the top of the world rankings. She surpassed her compatriot Chris Evert, who had held that rank for 113 consecutive weeks between May 1976 and July 1978.

In Madrid, she lost her first match of the season to Petra Kvitová in two sets (2-6, 3-6) in the semifinals and one hour and 13 minutes of play. She had eliminated in the second round the young Madison Brengle (6-0, 6-1) and Victoria Azarenka after saving three match points (7-6[5] , 3-

6, 7-6^1) in a match of pure madness, where to find a success of Serena Williams after having saved match points, we must go back to Sydney 2009

In Rome, where she was the two-time defending champion, she was forced to withdraw just after her second round win over Anastasia Pavlyuchenkova (6-1, 6-3) due to an elbow injury sustained in Madrid the week before.

On June 6, she won for the third time the French Open and her 20^e Grand Slam against the Czech Lucie Šafářová after more than 2 hours of hard struggle (6-3, 6^2 -7, 6-2). To do this, she fought almost the entire fortnight: in the second round against the German Anna-Lena Friedsam (5-7, 6-3, 6-3), in the third round against Victoria Azarenka (3-6, 6-4, 6-2) really playing with fire, and in the fourth round three points from defeat she defeated not without difficulty the young Sloane Stephens (1-6, 7-5, 6-3). Then in the semifinals, while she is sick, she defeats the Swiss Timea Bacsinszky 24^e world, (4-6, 6-3, 6-0) in almost two hours. In the final, she reversed the trend at 0-2 in the third set to win (6-3, 6^2 -7, 6-2). She is the first player to win the first two majors of the season since Jennifer Capriati in 2001 .

She then won the third Grand Slam of the season at Wimbledon by beating Spain's Garbiñe Muguruza, 20^e , in the final (6-4, 6-4) in an hour and a half, which was her first major final . She previously lost a set to Heather Watson (6-2, 4-6, 7-5) in the third round going just short of the exit, then dismissed her sister Venus in the round of 16 in two sets. From the quarters, she faced Victoria Azarenka slowly coming back to a good level (3-6, 6-2, 6-3) but will win against her, despite much more difficulties and more than two hours, and the Russian Maria Sharapova in the semis (6-2, 6-4) in only 1h19, showing her supremacy. This is her 6^e title at Wimbledon and her 21^e Grand Slam title. She also achieves the Grand Slam over two years, being the title holder of the four major tournaments. These two series twelve years apart (she achieved the same feat in 2002-2003) have earned the name *Serena Slam* .

In Båstad, she was forced to forfeit her first round match and skip Stanford because of an elbow injury that had been bothering her since Madrid. As of July 20, she reached the 250^e week at the top of the world rankings, the fourth highest total behind Graf, Navratilova and Evert.

In Toronto, she lost only her second match of the season, advancing to the semifinals despite an average serve against the young Belinda Bencic with a score of : 6-3, 5-7, 4-6.

She won her fifth title of the season in Cincinnati by eliminating world number three Simona Halep in the final: 6-3, 7-6^5 , where the only player to take a set from her on this week was Ana Ivanović in the quarterfinals. By defending her title, she becomes the first player to win this tournament twice.

At the US Open, three-time defending champion Serena Williams has the opportunity to achieve the first one-year Grand Slam of tennis since Steffi Graf in 1988 and join her with 22 Grand Slam singles titles in the Open era. After a difficult third round against Bethanie Mattek-Sands, not far from exiting, then eliminating her sister Venus in the quarterfinals in three sets (6-2, 1-6, 6-3) in 1 hour and 40 minutes in a beautiful match. She surprisingly fell in the semifinals on September 11, to Italian Roberta Vinci, then 43^e world player (6-2, 4-6, 4-6) in just two hours of play· . Between 2011 and 2015, all eight of Serena Williams' Grand Slam losses were to players ranked outside the top 10 in the WTA rankings.

To everyone's surprise, she ended her season by withdrawing from the Beijing tournament and the Masters, where she was the three-time title holder. However, she had an exceptional season with 5 titles, including three Grand Slams, and finished the season once again at the top of the WTA rankings.

2016 - Two Grand Slam finals lost, 22^e Grand Slam title and 14^e in doubles

Serena Williams begins her 2016 season by defending her title at the Australian Open. She reaches the final without a hitch, beating Maria Sharapova in the quarterfinals for the 18^e times in a row, and in the semifinals the Polish Agnieszka Radwańska, giving her a good beating. There she faced Angelique Kerber 6^e world, who won the title after a disputed match (4-6, 6-3, 4-6) in more than two hours, where Williams made many mistakes with a gesture tense by the event· . And signifying her disappointment and incomprehension in a press conference.

Feverish, she was forced to withdraw from the Dubai and Doha tournaments. On February 8, Serena Williams dominates the WTA rankings for the 280^e week of her career and, more importantly, for the 157^e consecutive week, a mark that surpasses Martina Navrátilová's (156) and brings her closer to Steffi Graf (180).

A year after her return to the California desert, Serena Williams is back in action to try to become the first player to win the Indian Wells tournament for the third time. She won all her matches in two sets (after beating Simona Halep in the quarter and Agnieszka Radwańska in the semifinals, among others, who will have shown a good level) to reach the final against Victoria Azarenka, but lost (4-6, 4-6) in 1:28. In Miami the following week, she struggled to find her footwork as well as her serve and her mind. She was knocked out in the round of 16 by 19^e Svetlana Kuznetsova (7-6^3 , 1-6, 2-6) and ended her 20-match winning streak in Miami.

III, she skipped the tournament in Madrid and began the season on clay in Rome. She won her 70^e title and the 4^e in Rome against her compatriot Madison Keys (7-6^5 , 6-3) without losing a set, having beaten and taken revenge in the quarter against Svetlana Kuznetsova.

At the French Open tournament, she qualified for the final without any real surprise. But having struggled to beat Kristina Mladenovic in the third round, then the first surprise Yulia Putintseva 60^e world, losing a set in the quarters, and the Dutch Kiki Bertens in the semifinals, the other surprise (7-6^7 , 6-4) in 1 hour and 38 minutes in a match also tense. She lost (5-7, 4-6) in one hour and 43 minutes to the world's 4^e Garbiñe Muguruza, thus losing two consecutive Grand Slam finals . However, she becomes the same year the highest paid female sportswoman in the world ahead of Maria Sharapova and Ronda Rousey with 25.4 million euros in cumulative earnings over the last twelve months (from May 2015 to May 2016).

Her season on grass came down to defending her title at Wimbledon. She easily gets past qualifier Amra Sadiković in the first round, before being pushed around a bit by Christina McHale (6^7 -7, 6-2, 6-4) in the second round. She then easily advanced to the round of 16, and in the process signed her 300^e career Grand Slam victory. The next day (July 4), she began her 300^e week at the top of the world rankings. In the next three matches, she faced three Russians, Svetlana Kuznetsova, seeded No.^{o} 13 (7-5, 6-0), who she beat severely in the second set, and Anastasia Pavlyuchenkova, seeded No.^{o} 21 in the quarters, whom she defeated (6-4, 6-4) in one hour and 13 minutes without being troubled. In the semifinals, she beat the surprise of the tournament, Elena Vesnina (6-2, 6-0) in 48 minutes (17 minutes for the last set). She reached the final for the third consecutive time in Grand Slam this season where she faced the world n° 4 Angelique Kerber, for the rematch of the final of the Australian Open. She won the final (7-5, 6-3) in one hour and 21 minutes and became a legend by equaling Steffi Graf's mark with a 22[e] major title» . A few hours later, she and her sister Venus won the doubles for the 6[e] time in their careers by beating (6-3, 6-4) the pair Tímea Babos/Yaroslava Shvedova in one hour and 27 minutes. They now have 14 Grand Slam victories in as many finals played (no losses).

She then withdrew from the Montreal tournament due to an inflammation of the right shoulder. She will therefore start the Rio Olympics without any preparation tournament.

She returns for the Olympics in both singles and doubles with her sister Venus. In doubles, they lose to the surprise then seeded n° 1 in the first round (3-6, 4-6) against the Czech pair Lucie Šafářová / Barbora Strýcová while they were triple Olympic champions and undefeated at the Olympics together. In singles, she easily defeated Daria Gavrilova in two sets and then had more difficulty, especially in the first set against Alizé Cornet, beating her (7-6[5] , 6-2) in almost two hours. Finally, she faced the world's 20e Elina Svitolina in the third round, and lost in two sets (4-6, 3-6) by committing too many unforced errors (37 in total) and making five double faults in the same game at 3-4 in the second set. Then double title holder at the Cincinnati tournament, Serena withdraws because of an inflammation in her right shoulder contracted before the Olympic Games.

At the US Open, the last Grand Slam tournament of the year, she easily defeated Ekaterina Makarova (6-3, 6-3), the American Vania King (6-2, 6-1) and Yaroslava Shvedova (6-2, 6-3) to reach the quarterfinals. There she faced Simona Halep, whom she beat with much more difficulty, losing the second set (6-2, 4-6, 6-3), which made her very tired afterwards. She reached the semi-final against Karolína Plíšková 11[e] to qualify for a new final and maybe win a 23^e Grand Slam tournament to overtake Steffi Graf. But she lost this semi-final, losing the first set (2-6, 6^5 -7) in 1h25 in total. The victory of the German Angelique Kerber in the semifinals also makes her lose at the end of the tournament her place as world number 1, which she had held continuously since February 2013.

For the Asian tour, because of her injuries, she withdraws for Wuhan and Beijing, hoping to return for the Singapore Masters. She ended up withdrawing from the Singapore Masters, still with a shoulder injury.

It was a mixed season for the American champion with one Grand Slam title and one Premier 5 title. She had not played so little since 2006.

2017 - Record number of Grand Slam wins in singles (23) and maternity

After four months without competition, Serena Williams begins the year 2017 with the tournament in Auckland. She won the first round against the French Pauline Parmentier (6-3, 6-4), but was defeated in the next round by her compatriot Madison Brengle then 72^e world (4-6, 7-6, 4-6).

She continues her season with the Australian Open. She does not lose a set in her journey to Melbourne where she reaches the final beating Belinda Bencic, Lucie Šafářová, Nicole Gibbs, Barbora Strýcová, then the 9^e world Johanna Konta in 1 hour and 15 minutes and finally, the returnee Mirjana Lučić-Baroni in only 50 minutes. She met her sister Venus Williams for the 28^e times on the WTA tour since 1998, for the eighth time in the final of a Grand Slam tournament, and for the first time since Wimbledon 2009. Serena won (6-4, 6-4) in 1 hour and 22 minutes in a match that she dominated completely. Serena Williams won her seventh Australian Open and 23rd Grand Slam singles tournament of her career, making her the record holder of Open titles ahead of Steffi Graf and one win away from the overall record in women's tennis history held by Margaret Smith Court. The American player won in Melbourne on January 28, 2017 at 35 years and 4 months, also becoming the oldest player to win this trophy during the Open era. In addition, this success allows her to regain the position of n° 1 in the world. She said: "I congratulate Venus, she is an incredible person. I would never have reached 23 without her, she inspires me, she is the main reason why I am here. So thank you Venus. Every time I saw you win during the fortnight, I thought I had to win too. I'm sure she'll be here next year." .

Serena Williams was forced to withdraw from the Indian Wells and Miami tournaments due to knee pain, resulting in the loss of her world number one ranking.

Without playing a single tournament, on April 24, she will once again top the WTA rankings. This is due to the fact that the Stuttgart tournament is held one week later than last year. Angelique Kerber, currently ranked No.$^\circ$ in the world, loses the 470 points she earned from her victory last year. The following week, on May 1er , she still retains the world ranking of 1er due to the early elimination of Angelique Kerber in her opening match in Stuttgart.

On April 19, she announced through her agent that she is expecting a child with her fiancé Alexis Ohanian, ending her season . She also assures that she intends to return to the courts after her pregnancy. On 1er September, at the maternity hospital in West Palm Beach (Florida), Serena Williams gives birth to a baby girl named Alexis Olympia Ohanian Jr. Serena Williams and Alexis Ohanian get married in New Orleans on November 16, 2017.

2018: return to competition, finals at Wimbledon and the US Open

In preparation for the 2018 season, Serena makes her return on December 30, at the Abu Dhabi exhibition tournament. She lost to the young Jeļena Ostapenko, n° 7 in the world and winner of the 2017 French Open in three sets (2-6, 6-3, [5-10]). Not feeling physically fit enough, she then gave up participating and defending her title at the Australian Open. She then decided to make her return to the circuit at the Fed Cup on February 10 against the Netherlands. She played with her sister in the doubles match, which they lost.

At the Indian Wells tournament, she went through the first and second rounds without losing a set against Zarina Diyas and Kiki Bertens before meeting up with her sister Venus in the 3^e round. 17 years after the fiasco of a semi-final that was not played, the confrontation with her elder sister ended in a defeat in two sets (3-6, 4-6). In Miami, she was soundly defeated in the first round 6-3, 6-2 by the young Japanese Naomi Osaka, who had just won the Indian Wells tournament.

She made her return to the Grand Slam at the 2018 French Open where she qualified for the round of 16. Unfortunately, she was forced to forfeit due to right pectoral pain, preventing her from serving. This is the first time in her career that the former world number 1 has had to forfeit a competition.

She made a stunning comeback at Wimbledon by reaching the final, losing only one set (to Camila Giorgi of Italy). However, she lost to Angelique Kerber in two sets (3-6, 3-6). She jumped 153 places in the WTA rankings the following week, from 183^e to 28 .^{e}

At the San Jose tournament, she was beaten in the first round by the British Johanna Konta in two quick sets (1-6, 0-6), the worst defeat of her career.

She withdrew two days before the start of the Montreal tournament (Canada tournament) for "personal reasons".

Then qualified for the 2e round of the Cincinnati tournament she lost to the Czech Petra Kvitová in three sets (3-6, 6-2, 3-6).

At the U.S. Open, the same scenario was played out as at Wimbledon; she lost only one set in the round of 16 to Estonia's Kaia Kanepi (6-0, 4-6, 6-3) and advanced to her 31e final at the U.S. Open against Japan's Naomi Osaka. This final was marked by several controversies: following three warnings from the chair umpire, the American was given a penalty game at 3-4 in the second set, giving her opponent a chance to close the match at 5-3. She was finally defeated in two sets (6-2, 6-4) and once again missed the opportunity to equal Margaret Court's record of 24 Grand Slam titles .

She finished the year at the 16e world ranking in singles.

On October 19, 2018, she received the WTA *Comeback of the* Year Award.

2019: back in the top 10, finals at Wimbledon and the US Open

Serena Williams starts her year with the 31^e edition of the Hopman Cup. She won all three of her singles matches, beating Greece's María Sákkari (7-6^3 , 6-2), Switzerland's Belinda Bencic (4-6, 6-4, 6-3) and Great Britain's Katie Boulter (6-1, 7-6^2), but she and her partner Frances Tiafoe did not win any of their three doubles matches. They finish last in their pool. On January 1er 2019, she meets in mixed doubles, for the first time since the beginning of her career, her male alter-ego, the Swiss Roger Federer. The Swiss take the lead over the Americans (4-2, 4-3^3) but their meeting marks this edition of the Hopman Cup.

She makes her return to the Australian Open after her victory in 2017. She advances to the quarterfinals after beating Germany's Tatjana Maria (6-0, 6-2), Canada's Eugenie Bouchard (6-2, 6-2), Ukraine's Dayana Yastremska (6-2, 6-1) and then finally the world's n° 1, Romania's Simona Halep, in three sets (6-1, 4-6, 6-4). This is the first time since 2012 that she beats the world number 1. She was finally defeated by the Czech Karolína Plíšková in three very close sets (4-6, 6-4, 5-7) and where she had four match points that she could not convert (at 5-1, then three times at 5-4), due to, among other things, a sprained ankle that appeared during the third set.

Taking advantage of the withdrawal of Denmark's Caroline Wozniacki from the Doha tournament, Serena Williams is back in the top 10 at No. 10, just 11 months after her return to competition.

She then participated in the Indian Wells tournament. Taking advantage of her seeded status, she plays her first match in the second round. She played against the Belarusian Victoria Azarenka. The match is of great intensity, reminiscent of the best matches of two players against each other, and is finally won by the American (7-5, 6-3). She then faced the Spaniard Garbine Muguruza. Leading 1 set to 0 and 1-0 in the second set, she was forced to retire. The tournament confirms that the player was ill a few hours after her withdrawal from the court. Her return to Mimai is again shortened by a left knee injury. However, she won her first match against the Swedish Rebecca Peterson with difficulty (6-3, 1-6, 6-1).

Her knee injury compromises her clay court season. However, in preparation for Roland Garros, she entered the tournament in Rome. She won her first match without too much difficulty against the Swedish Rebecca Peterson (6-4, 6-2) but had to withdraw again due to her knee. She had to meet her sister Venus.

Her return to the courts is made at Roland Garros. Her first match is chaotic but she wins against the Russian Vitalia Diatchenko (2-6, 6-1, 6-0). She then defeated the Japanese Kurumi Nara (6-3, 6-2) but was finally eliminated in the 3e round by her compatriot Sofia Kenin (2-6, 5-7). She then said she wanted to rest and heal before returning to Wimbledon.

Wishing to play more matches, Serena decided to play singles and mixed doubles with Andy Murray. In mixed doubles, she reached the round of 16. Her first match against Alexa Guarachi and Andreas Mies made history as the earliest scheduled doubles match in the competition on center court. Together with Andy Murray, they won (6-4, 6-1) and repeated in the second round against Raquel Atawo and Fabrice Martin (7-5, 6-3). They finally lost in their third match against the seeds n° 1 Nicole Melichar and Bruno Soares (3-6, 6-4, 2-6). In singles, she reached the final again after defeating Italy's Giulia Gatto-Monticone (6-2, 7-5), Slovenia's Kaja Juvan (2-6, 6-2, 6-4), Germany's Julia Görges (6-3, 6-4), Spain's Carla Suárez Navarro (6-2, 6-2),

America's Alison Riske (6-4, 4-6, 6-3) and Czech Republic's Barbora Strýcová (6-1, 6-2). She again missed the opportunity to win her 24^e Major by losing to Romanian Simona Halep (2-6, 2-6).

In preparation for the US Open, she is taking part in the Rogers Cup. Taking advantage of Petra Kvitová's forfeit, she was one of the eight seeds to benefit from a first round bye. She began the competition in the second round. She first defeated Belgian Elise Mertens (6-3, 6-3) and then Russian Ekaterina Alexandrova (7-5, 6-4). In the quarter-finals, she met the Japanese Naomi Osaka and took her revenge from the previous US Open by winning the match (6-3, 6-4). She then met the Czech surprise of the tournament, Marie Bouzková, who surprised her by winning the first set 6-1 but which she finally mastered (1-6, 6-3, 6-3) to qualify for her 96^e final in her career, her fifth in the tournament. She will face local Bianca Andreescu. Caught by back spasms, she gave up in the first set, down 3-1. She then withdrew from the Cincinnati tournament.

At the US Open, the same scenario presented itself to her as the previous edition: she qualified for the final. To do this, she passes the Russian Maria Sharapova (6-1, 6-1), the American Catherine McNally (5-7, 6-3, 6-1), the Czech Karolína Muchová (6-3, 6-2), the Croatian Petra Martić (6-3, 6-4), the Chinese Wang Qiang (6-1, 6-0) and the Ukrainian Elina Svitolina (6-3, 6-1). She fell again in the final, this time to Canadian Bianca Andreescu (3-6, 5-7). She thus puts an end to her season by not participating in the second round of the Masters, even though she is qualified for it.

She finished the season at 10^e in singles.

At the end of the year, she was voted best athlete of the decade by the Associated Press.

2020 - 2021: title in Auckland and exit from the top 40

To start the season, Serena enters the Auckland tournament. Seeded No.° 1, she eliminated Italian Camila Giorgi (6-3, 6-2), American Christina McHale (3-6, 6-2, 6-3), German Laura Siegemund (6-4, 6-3) and American Amanda Anisimova (6-1, 6-1). Qualified for the final, she was badly beaten in the first games by her compatriot Jessica Pegula (1-3) but finally emerged victorious, winning her 73^e title and her first title since 2017 (6-3, 6-4). She took advantage of the presence of her friend at the tournament, Denmark's Caroline Wozniacki, to also enter the doubles draw. Together they reached the final but were defeated by the Muhammad-Townsend pair (4-6, 4-6). Her victory made even more history: she became the only player to win a singles title in four different decades. At the end of the tournament, she announced that she would donate her entire prize money to the victims of the fires in Australia.

At the Australian Open, she began her 24^e Grand Slam as the top seeded player (°). She started with a victory in less than an hour over Russian Anastasia Potapova (6-0, 6-3). She then eliminated the Slovenian Tamara Zidanšek (6-2, 6-3). She was finally surprised by the Chinese Wang Qiang who eliminated her in the 3^e round, during a match in 3 sets (4-6, 7-6^2 , 5-7).

On January 15, 2020, she is officially selected for the qualification phase of the Fed Cup, 2 years after her last appearance. Against Latvia, February 7-8, she is lined up by captain Kathy Rinaldi on the singles. She defeated Jeḷena Ostapenko (7-6^4 , 7-6^3) but lost to Anastasija Sevastova (6^5 -7, 6-2, 6^4 -7). At the U.S. Open, she was seeded No. 3 and passed Sloane Stephens (2-6, 6-2, 62) and Maria Sakkari (6-3, 6-7, 6-3). She reached the semifinals where she was defeated 1-6, 6-3, 6-3 by Victoria Azarenka.

2021 is a year in which Serena gets no title and no final. She reached the semi-finals twice. The first at the Yarra Valley Classic (forfeit to Ashleigh Barty) and the second lost heavily to Naomi Osaka at the Australian Open (6-3, 6-4) after beating Simona Halep (6-3, 6-3) and Aryna Sabalenka (6-4, 2-6, 6-4) among others.

She suffered a bitter failure against Elena Rybakina at Roland Garros in the 1/8 finals (beaten 6-3, 7-5), and especially against Aliaksandra Sasnovich at Wimbledon, forced to abandon in the first round after a fall. She left the court in tears, but to the applause of the public. She finishes her season ranked 41^e in the world, losing 30 places in one year.

2022: worst ranking apart from maternity

In 2022, Serena loses 200 places in the rankings as she goes from 41^e to 241^e in the world in February, this is due to the absence of a match since Wimbledon 2021.

In an interview with *Entertainment Tonight*, Serena said, "*I've been preparing for this day, in fact I've been preparing for over a decade. If you've seen* King Richard, you *know that my dad told me that I had to prepare for anything, so that's what I did. At the end of the day, I think it's really important to have a plan and that's what I've always had.*"

Awards

For summary tables:

- 0 : *at least one participation in the category and on the surface*
- - : *no participation*
- total number of titles (total number of titles inside)

In women's singles

Serena Williams has won **73** titles including **23** Grand Slam singles titles. She is the 5[e] most successful player of the Open Era and holds the most Grand Slam titles.

Serena Williams has lost **25** singles finals in her career:

In women's doubles

Serena Williams has won **23** doubles titles, including **14** Grand Slam titles, all with her older sister Venus Williams. This makes them the 2[e] (ex-aequo with Natasha Zvereva & Gigi Fernández) best women's doubles pair of the Grand Slam era.

Periods at the number one position in the world

With 319 weeks at the top of the WTA rankings, Serena Williams is the 3[oe] player to have spent the most time at No. 1 in the world after Steffi Graf (377 weeks) and Martina Navrátilová (332 weeks). She co-holds the record with Steffi Graf for the most consecutive weeks spent at the top of the rankings with 186 weeks.

Course in major competitions

Serena Williams holds the record (tied with Steffi Graf) of **29** major singles titles (23 Grand Slams, 5 Masters and 1 Olympic Games). Below are her results in major tournaments by year:

In "Premier Mandatory" and "Premier 5

The WTA Premier Mandatory and Premier 5 tournaments (between 2009 and 2020) and the WTA 1000 (from 2021 onwards) are the most prestigious event categories after the four Grand Slam events.

In Fed Cup

Career highlights and records

- Serena is the 5th^e player in history to win all 4 Grand Slam tournaments in singles and doubles (after Doris Hart, Shirley Fry, Margaret Court and Martina Navrátilová) and the 1st^{re} to win all 4 Grand Slam tournaments and the Olympic gold (called "Golden Grand Slam") in singles and doubles career
- She is the 3^e player in history (after Helen Willis in 1924 and Venus Williams in 2000) to win Olympic gold in singles and doubles in the same year (2012).

In single

- Second player to win the Masters *(created in 1972)* from her 1re participation *(in 2001)*, after Chris Evert, winner of the first edition.

- She won a grand slam tournament without being seeded, ranked n° 81 on the WTA at the beginning of the 2007 Australian Open.
- Only player to have won 3 grand slams by saving match points:
    - 2 match points in the semi-finals against Kim Clijsters at the 2003 Australian Open
    - 3 match points in the semi-finals against Maria Sharapova at the 2005 Australian Open
    - 1 match point in the semi-finals against Elena Dementieva at Wimbledon in 2009.
- By winning the Australian Open in 2003, she became the 6^e player *(Open era)* to achieve
- She holds the record *(Open era)* of 6 US Open titles *(with Chris Evert)*.
- She holds the record *(Open era)* of 7 titles at the Australian Open
- She is the only person in history *(men and women)* to have won three of the Grand Slam singles tournaments at least six times.
- She is the only person in history *(men and women)* to have won at least 10 grand slam singles titles over two decades *(10 from 2000 to 2009 and 11 since 2010)*.
- 2^e player in history *(after Martina Navrátilová)* to win Grand Slam singles titles in 3 different decades: 1990's, 2000's and 2010's.
- The only player in the Open Era to win more than 60 matches in every Grand Slam singles tournament.
- Oldest player in history to hold all 4 grand slam singles tournaments *(33 years and 11 months before the start of the 2015 US Open)*.
- Only person *(men and women)* to have achieved a career golden grand slam after 30 years *(Wimbledon in 2012, Olympic gold in 2012, US*

Open in 2012, Roland Garros in 2013 and Australian Open in 2015).

- At the 2016 US Open, Williams achieved her 308[e] career grand slam singles victory, the best mark in the history of men and women combined: Martina Navrátilová counting her 306 wins and Roger Federer her 307.

In duplicate

Note: Serena Williams only plays doubles with her older sister Venus during Grand Slam tournaments. All the facts and records are about this pair.

- By winning the Australian Open in 2001, they became the 5th[e] pair to complete a career grand slam in tennis history and the 1st[re] to complete the golden grand slam.
- 1[re] pair in history (men and women combined) to achieve a golden double Grand Slam in their career: Australian Open in 2001 and 2003, French Open in 1999 and 2010, Wimbledon in 2000 and 2002, US Open in 1999 and 2009 and Olympic gold in 2000 and 2008
- The only pair in history (men and women combined) to have 3 Olympic titles.

Awards

- Champion of the world champions by the newspaper L'Équipe in 2012, 2013 and 2015.
- Sportswoman of the Year by the Laureus Foundation in 2003, 2010, 2016 and 2018.

Personal life

Serena Williams gets engaged to Alexis Ohanian, co-founder of Reddit, on December 29, 2016. On 1er September 2017, Serena Williams gave birth to her first child named Alexis Olympia Ohanian Jr. She married Alexis Ohanian on November 16, 2017 in New Orleans, Louisiana, in a low-key ceremony with the presence of a shower of stars including singer Beyoncé, reality TV star Kim Kardashian and actress Eva Longoria among others.

In 2004, she created her own clothing brand under the name of **Aneres** (Serena in reverse) and in 2018, a new brand called this time **Serena**.

See all our published books here:
https://campsite.bio/unitedlibrary

CPSIA information can be obtained
at www.ICGtesting.com
Printed in the USA
BVHW051717140223
658500BV00024B/604